BUILDING A GREEN ECONOMY

THE ECONOMICS OF CARBON PRICING
& THE TRANSITION TO CLEAN, RENEWABLE FUELS

Securing the nation's economy and environment against the corrosive impacts of burning carbon-based fuels requires a concerted nationwide effort, rooted in sound policy and bold incentives, to steer the nation's energy markets toward more sustainable, clean and renewable resources for power generation. This document explains how this transition can be achieved quickly and without negatively impacting the personal wealth of the average American household.

SEPTEMBER 2010

CITIZENS CLIMATE LOBBY
www.citizensclimatelobby.org

Building a Green Economy
The Economics of Carbon Pricing & the Transition to Clean,
Renewable Fuels

ISBN: 978-0-9826491-7-6

Report prepared by Joseph Robertson

With the generous collaboration of the following CCL partners:
Amy Hoyt Bennett, Mark Reynolds, Marshall Saunders, Todd
Smith, Antoinette Stein, and Steve Valk

CCL Contacts

Steve Valk, media: steve.valk@citizensclimatelobby.org
Joseph Robertson, author: jr@thehotspring.net

TABLE OF CONTENTS

EXECUTIVE SUMMARY

Putting a price on carbon creates a contextual incentive for diversification and innovation in the energy economy. When Germany shifted its tax-base from income to energy, it spurred a decade of aggressive public and private investment in renewable resources. In just four years, it became the world leader in clean energy export, taking 70% of the world market just eight years after the initial policy shift.

German firms are driving investments of €400 billion in the Desertec solar project in North Africa, part of a plan to connect two continents via multi-gigawatt undersea transmission cables and advanced smart-grid technology. The project will revolutionize the energy sector in Europe and Africa, creating wealth for businesses and communities large and small. Morocco, for instance, plans to use its desert and mountain terrain, as well as its wind-intensive coastal areas, to generate enough renewable energy to become an export leader for the European market. This model can be duplicated in mountainous, desert-rich and coastal states across the U.S.

Concerns that coal country will be adversely affected by a price on carbon are understandable but somewhat unfounded. Communities dependent on coal for employment are not generally more prosperous than the national average, so a transition to clean renewable resources can help to overcome problems of endemic persistent poverty. Studies comparing cost-benefit analysis for mountaintop removal mining and wind energy show wind is more effective at generating prosperity over the long term, for all but a narrow group of interests.

The regional disparity in impact from a carbon tax is projected to be negligible, starting at just two-thirds of one percent and moving to just one-third of one percent over time. If revenue from

5

a carbon fee is returned to all households, any wider regional disparity might be reduced by targeted dividend adjustments. Communities in remote areas, or which rely on coal for cheap energy or for employment, can benefit economically from diversifying into and taking ownership of clean renewable-energy technologies.

Job creation will be the hallmark of the clean energy revolution. Studies show the potential for millions of new jobs in industries ranging from manufacturing to installation and maintenance, as well as administration, marketing, energy efficiency and other related fields. The potential for efficiency gains from clean-energy and smart-grid technologies will free up massive amounts of consumer spending over time and relieve dependence on fossil fuels from hostile states.

CARBON PRICING IMPACT PROJECTIONS

VARIATIONS BY REGION

One of the key concerns in any program designed to put a price on carbon dioxide emissions is who will be most heavily affected by the resulting cost increase. It is generally expected that lower-income households and communities will see the biggest impact. Gasoline, electricity and home heating tend to consume a larger percentage of their income than they do for the wealthy. Unlike businesses, individuals and families don't enjoy a tax write-off for such expenses.

Regional variations in wealth distribution and energy consumption are also a concern in crafting responsible legislation. As the Carbon Tax Center reports:

> *Electricity rates in the Pacific Northwest, which is generously endowed with hydro-electric power, should scarcely be affected by carbon emissions pricing through either a tax or cap-and-trade system. In contrast, the Plains states, which primarily employ coal for electricity generation, and the Northeastern states, which rely heavily on fuel oil for heating, could face disproportionate impacts. In addition, people in rural areas tend to drive longer distances than city-dwellers, so their transportation costs would be expected to rise more.[1]*

How diverse are the impacts to regions, industries, states, communities and households? The Carbon Tax Center (CTC) cites a study by the American Enterprise Institute (AEI), which examined the projected impact of a carbon fee.

---

[1] Carbon Tax Center, "Regional Disparities", 2009.

The AEI working paper, "The Incidence of a U.S. Carbon Tax: A Lifetime and Regional Analysis"[2], published January 2008, finds that:

> *The maximum difference in the average rate across regions is less than two-thirds of a percentage point in 1987. The maximum difference rises to 0.9 percentage points in 1997 and then falls to just over one-third of a percentage point in 2003. It is quite remarkable how small the differences are across the regions given the variation in weather conditions and driving patterns across the regions.*

Why so little difference? Most of the economic impact of any carbon pricing system is likely to filter back to consumers through the entire consumer goods economy, not through direct consumption of carbon-based fuels. AEI examined both the *direct* and *indirect* components of a carbon tax system. Direct is consumption of gasoline, electricity and home heating fuel; indirect is the cost of other goods and services.

The authors of the AEI study found that while there is reason for concern about "uneven regional effects" from a carbon tax:

> *We report the average carbon tax paid per household across regions and find that the regional variation is at best modest. By 2003 variation across regions is sufficiently small that one could argue that a carbon tax is distributionally neutral across regions.*[3]

The AEI paper also finds "the variation across regions is relatively modest with the variation decreasing over time."[4] An

---

[2] Hassett, et al., p. 13.

[CCL NOTE: Footnote citations which list only author or organization and page number or date are, like all references in these footnotes, references to works cited in the References section at the end of this document. URLs are included for all sources for which they exist.]

[3] Hassett, et al., p. 3.

[4] Hassett, et al., p. 15.

economy-wide shift toward clean energy sources accounts, in part, for this trend.

Another study, which took a less nuanced approach but looked at a wider range of data, sought to evaluate and compare five different scenarios for pricing carbon dioxide emissions. In its report, *The Incidence of U.S. Climate Policy: Alternative Uses of Revenues From a Cap-and-Trade Auction,* Resources for the Future (RFF) found that variation across regions may be more significant if the variation is measured both across regions and throughout various socio-economic strata at once.

Whereas the AEI study examined the incidence of a carbon tax over the span of a lifetime of income and across diverse regions, the RFF approach focused more on what can be done with the revenue generated from a cap-and-trade system, and views the cap-and-trade model as a proxy for other more direct carbon taxation proposals. The analysis is conducted with the understanding that the price per metric ton of CO_2 emissions can be set, for any carbon cap or carbon tax system, at a constant, predictable cost of \$20.87.

> *Some earlier literature has concluded that regional differences from CO2 pricing policies are likely to be relatively small (Hassett et al. 2009). We find that the range of impacts on an average household can be as high as \$231. For example, we find that a CO2 price of \$20.87 implemented with revenues returned to households as taxable dividends yields a loss in consumer surplus of \$234 per year for the average household in the Northeast, but the average household in Texas loses only \$3 per year. The loss in consumer surplus for the average household on a national basis would be \$86.*[5]

Burtraw, Sweeney and Walls, agreed with the AEI analysis, concluding from the above figures that "When expressed as a fraction of income, these differences are quite small."[6] This does

---

[5] Burtraw, et al., ps. 2-3.

[6] Burtraw, et al., p. 3.

not, however, mean there is no potential for noteworthy variation in impact from a carbon-pricing scheme. Their report for RFF found that "consumer surplus losses [resulting from carbon-pricing policies] can be quite high" among poorer households and communities, because poorer consumers pay a much higher percentage of their income to buy the same amount of energy.

But devoting revenues from the carbon-pricing —in this case a cap-and-trade program— to dividends returned directly to consumers can actually make even the regressive impact on poor households and communities progressive. RFF found that when a dividend is introduced, to complement the carbon-pricing program in question, "average households in the lowest two deciles may enjoy a consumer surplus gain of as much as 5.4 percent of income (in Texas) or of just 1.9 percent of income (in the Northeast)."[7]

Though the impact variation is not projected to amount to more than 2% of total annual income, even in poor communities, the Carbon Tax Center proposes adjusting dividends to deal with regional disparities:

> *For instance, if households in the Pacific Northwest would indeed pay less in carbon taxes than the national average, individuals or households in that region would receive proportionately lesser payroll tax reductions or direct distributions of revenue. Households in the Plains states might receive a correspondingly greater share of the recycled revenue. In this way, a revenue-neutral carbon tax could be regional-neutral as well.*[8]

The key to addressing regional disparities, or shepherding coal-dependent communities through the transition, is to mitigate costs and create employment opportunities over the short to medium term. Returning revenue from carbon pricing to every American household is one way to address the problem of cost.

---

[7] Burtraw, et al., p. 3.

[8] Carbon Tax Center, "Regional Disparities", 2009.

Another is to focus incentives for energy and infrastructure investment on communities that have a longer road to travel from carbon-based to clean energy.[9]

ECONOMIC OPPORTUNITY: ENERGY INNOVATION

A transition in energy sourcing must and will bring a shift in economic opportunity for communities closely tied to carbon-based energy. Communities in coal-rich areas are often tied economically to coal production and energy consumption elsewhere. But studies show that this does not necessarily translate into healthier economies in dependent communities.

A SourceWatch report finds that:

There are 54 coal mines in the U.S. that produced more than 4 million tons of coal in 2006; these 54 mines are located in 34 counties. The median 2005 poverty rate in these 34 counties was 15.5% - 17% higher than the U.S. average of 13.3%. The median 2000 per capita income in these 34 counties was $16,246 - 25% lower than the U.S. average of $21,587.[10]

The same report showed that in 2000, income levels were 15% lower than the national average in counties where 404 coal-fired plants capable of more than 100MW of power generation were located. A report published in June 2010 examined the overall cost of the coal industry to Tennessee taxpayers. It found that for each of the three counties that "produce substantial amounts of coal... coal jobs accounted for approximately 1% of total employment in these counties."[11]

---

[9] The dividend itself, if distributed on a numerically equal per-capita basis, can be a vehicle for that incentives shift, because the amount received will equate to a significantly higher percentage of total annual income among poor households and communities than among the more affluent.

[10] SourceWatch. "Coal and Jobs in the United States".

[11] McIlmoil, et al., Tennessee, p. 43.

Even in West Virginia, where the coal industry may be the leading employer in many communities, it does not account for a majority of employment or economic activity. The coal industry directly employs approximately 21,012 West Virginia residents, 3% of total employment. Adding to that an estimated 47,531 jobs indirectly related to coal production, the coal industry accounts for as much as 9% of jobs in West Virginia — an important figure but not a majority. [12]

While coal provides roughly 8% of in-state tax revenues for West Virginia, a report on the impact of coal on the state's budget found "that total tax revenues related to direct employment in the coal industry amounted to approximately $125.5 million. However, state expenditures to support those employees amounted to approximately $125.9 million."[13] Downstream Strategies' analysis of the impact of coal on the West Virginia state budget found total fiscal activity in FY2009 amounted to a net-cost to the state of $97.5 million.[14]

Coal-dependent communities could benefit from a transition to clean, renewable fuels, which could produce safer, more reliable jobs, and an expandable energy economy capable of raising income levels. Comparative analysis[15] shows a developed renewable resources industry could provide far better fiscal returns to the county and the state than coal presently does, while raising wages and expanding overall employment opportunity.

---

[12] McIlmoil, et al., West Virginia, p. 57.

[13] McIlmoil, et al., West Virginia, p. xii.

[14] McIlmoil, et al., West Virginia, p. 59.

[15] "The wind scenario would generate significantly more local taxes for Raleigh County than the mountaintop removal scenario. Only about $36,000 per year in coal severance taxes would be paid to Raleigh County by mountaintop removal mining on Coal River Mountain. In comparison, a wind farm would generate about $1.74 million in local property taxes each year. While the severance taxes end when mining ends, the property taxes from the wind farm will continue into the future." — Hansen, et al., p. 45.

CASE STUDIES

GERMANY: WORLD LEADER IN WIND POWER, JOB-CREATION ENGINE

In 1999, Germany implemented a much-needed power-generation transition plan, to start the move from limited-reserve carbon-based fuels to clean renewable resources. Over four years, from 1999 to 2003, Germany shifted its tax sourcing from income to energy. As a result, annual CO_2 emissions fell an estimated 20 million metric tons —a 2.4% reduction, which continues to mount even after the carbon tax level stops rising— and in 2003, 250,000 jobs were created.[16]

Just four years into its carbon-focused tax shift, Germany led the world in wind energy manufacturing and export, and by 2006, it had come to control 70 percent of the global export market for wind-energy technology. Its photo-voltaic sector global export share for 2006 was 30 percent.[17]

German firms are positioned to surpass the clean energy investments of the European Union's total clean energy stimulus. For the Desertec solar project, a consortium of firms led by Munich Re, E.ON AG, Siemens and DeutscheBank, will invest €400 billion —16 times[18] the EU stimulus fund for clean energy. The project will build the world's most advanced and extensive solar power generation complex across North Africa,

---

[16] Knigge, et al., p. 8.

[17] *Solar Today*, June 2010 edition, p. 27.

[18] Boselli, May 27, 2010 — Green investment through economic stimulus at "about 25 billion euros ($30.70 billion) in the EU, according to the International Institute for Environment and Development."

complete with undersea cables for intercontinental transmission.[19]

Munich Re is one of the world's leading reinsurance companies —insuring insurers against catastrophic loss— so a key factor driving its investment in Desertec is the need to protect its business against "billions of euros in claims for damage caused by climate change in coming years," as reported by Reuters.[20] Germany's economy is now building long-term resilience by steering major investment into clean energy resources and a renewable energy transmission grid.

MOROCCO: RISING ENERGY EXPORTER

In part due to Europe's new focus on clean energy from the north African desert, Morocco shifted its industrial-export planning toward clean energy. Morocco's proximity to Europe and renewable desert resources allow for what may become a booming market in clean energy exports. The Desertec Foundation cites:

> An agreement between the EU and Morocco on a joint program of producing clean power from deserts (solar and wind) and transmission to Europe. The studies have demonstrated that solar power from the excellent sites in Morocco would be cheaper in Spain than from local solar power plants, including the costs of transmission. The same is true for the excellent wind sites in Morocco. Within 2 decades Spain and other parts of Europe could receive clean power from deserts at costs less than from their local fossil fuel power plants.[21]

Just one wind farm outside Tangiers was generating 140 MW of power from wind by January 2010, and another with 300 MW of generating capacity, near Tarfaya on the Atlantic coast, will come

---

[19] Reuters, June 16, 2009.

[20] Reuters, June 16, 2009.

[21] Desertec Foundation, p. 48.

online in 2011. The plan includes investment of $9 billion to build 2,000 MW of generating capacity from concentrated solar-thermal, which could generate up to 38% of Morocco's total energy supply by 2020 and "decrease its oil imports by 12 per cent, saving the country US$500–700 million annually." [22] Those savings allow for lower total costs of production and distribution, making clean energy a commodity Morocco can export, allowing for new investment and the further expansion of the clean energy production sector.

Morocco's first solar-thermal plant with 100 MW of capacity is expected to be commissioned by the end of 2010. Its national plan includes clean power-generation facilities (mainly wind and solar) and undersea transmission cables with more than 1 GW of capacity. Programs in industrial vocational training related to clean power construction, generation and maintenance are also planned.[23]

TEXAS: FROM OIL-DEPENDENT TO U.S. LEADER IN WIND ENERGY

Despite its history as an oil state, Texas leads the nation in wind-power generation, and is slated to rapidly expand its wind-power generation capacity. The statewide effort to scale up clean energy production from wind has led to an influx of investment and job creation. Texas now "generates more electricity from wind than any other state, had more than 55,000 clean energy economy jobs in 2007[24], and attracted more than $716 million in venture capital funds for clean technology between 2006 and 2008."[25]

---

[22] Boumedjout, 20 January 2010.

[23] Desertec Foundation, p. 49.

[24] For comparison, the Bureau of Labor Statistics report for August 2010 projects a national total of 166,800 jobs in the combined oil and natural gas extraction sector for August 2010. — BLS, Sept. 2010, p. 28.

[25] Pew, *The Clean Energy Economy*, p. 4.

Roscoe, Texas, a dying town, was transformed by over $1 billion in investment —starting in 2007— from Airtricity, an Irish wind power firm (now owned by German firm E.ON AG[26]). According to NPR, "income from a windmill is more dependable than dry-land cotton farming, where drought and hail are constant threats. Depending on the size of the turbine, a landowner can earn between $5,000 and $15,000 per windmill per year."[27]

Infrastructure development, including turbines, transmission lines and smart-grid technology, is crucial to accelerating the development of wind power resources. Investment is flowing into Oklahoma —which sits between two of the most wind-rich states in North America, Texas and Kansas— to open factories to serve the burgeoning wind energy market of the Great Plains.[28]

NEW JERSEY: RAPIDLY MOVED TO 2ND NATIONWIDE IN SOLAR POWER CAPACITY

Despite limited land area, New Jersey has rapidly moved into second place behind California in solar generating capacity. It achieved this by steering both state and federal incentives[29] toward installation of solar panels and implementing a renewable electricity standard.[30] The state plans to generate 3% of its electricity from solar power[31] and 12% from offshore wind by

---

[26] Reuters, October 4, 2007.

[27] Burnett, NPR, November 27, 2007.

[28] Gray, AWEA, June 30, 2010.

[29] NJCEP, "Renewable Energy Incentive Program Incentives", September 2010.

[30] The renewable electricity standard requires utilities to provide a minimum percentage of their overall supply by way of specified clean renewable energy technologies.

[31] That New Jersey is currently 2nd in the country in solar power generation, with plans to reach 3% solar power by 2020, is indicative of a persistent *underfunding* of solar power in U.S. energy markets. The scalability of solar power generation facilities is highly dependent on investment, as "reserves" far exceed total global demand and tech-

2020, when 30% of the state's electricity will come from carbon-free resources. [32]

The largest utility in the state began outfitting some 200,000 utility poles with solar panels in July 2009, part of a 40MW project it expects to complete by 2013.[33] It expanded its reach across the state with creative siting plans and grid-return royalty-sharing agreements. FedEx installed solar panels across 3 acres of roof-space on its Woodbridge, N.J., distribution hub, capable of generating 2.42 megawatts of clean electricity.

Incentives are crucial to New Jersey's success in deploying grid-tied solar power generation technologies:

New Jersey's $514 million program will double its solar capacity to 160 megawatts by 2013, and will be funded by utility customers. Costs will be defrayed slightly by a 30% federal tax credit, roughly $1 million a year in proceeds from the sale of solar renewable energy credits. In addition, solar energy fetches higher prices in the state's deregulated market, because it's produced at peak times.[34]

As of July 2010, the state's incentives program had delivered $331,856,370.88[35] in rebates for the installation of solar power-generation systems. Despite the economic downturn, New Jersey has seen its ability to capitalize and promote solar power installation continue to rise, partly due to federal incentives for economic recovery and clean-energy development, partly due to interest from private investors.

---

nologies are rapidly advancing in efficiency, output and distributive flexibility.

[32] Smith and Gold, *Wall Street Journal*, July 31, 2009.

[33] Sroka-Holzmann, *Courier News*, July 27, 2010.

[34] Smith and Gold, *Wall Street Journal*, July 31, 2009.

[35] NJCEP, "New Jersey Solar Installations by Year As of 7/31/10", August 2010.

NORTH CAROLINA: SOLAR NOW CHEAPER THAN NUCLEAR

In the state of North Carolina, solar power-generating resources are now able to provide cheaper electricity than planned new nuclear plants. While solar photo-voltaic installations enjoy subsidies that help make their cost competitive with established means of energy production, plans for new nuclear power plants require even greater subsidies than they have in the past, to be viable. A report, from the North Carolina Waste Awareness and Reduction Network and two Duke University researchers, finds that:

> *Now the nuclear industry is pressing for more subsidies. This is inappropriate. Commercial nuclear power has been with us for more than forty years. If it is not a mature industry by now, consumers of electricity should ask whether it ever will be competitive without public subsidies. There are no projections that nuclear electricity costs will decline.*[36]

Average costs per installed watt of energy generated from solar photo-voltaic systems declined from $12 in 1998 to just $8 in 2008. And efficiency gains from rapid advances in technology and materials have reduced costs another 25% in the last two years alone. While solar PV technology has seen power generation costs decline by 50% in just 12 years[37], nuclear power has become far more expensive than projections from just a few years ago suggested.

The cost of storing highly radioactive nuclear waste material has been escalating dramatically, since it was shown in federal court[38] that there is no proven means of securing the waste material for the length of time necessary to make a repository

---

[36] Blackburn and Cunningham, NC WARN, July 2010, p. 4.

[37] Blackburn and Cunningham, NC WARN, July 2010, p. 5.

[38] Eilperin, *Washington Post*, July 2004.

safe.[39] In fact, the escalating costs of planning and preparing for the installation of nuclear power stations has caused utilities to raise their rates, even in advance of having any new power generation capacity from nuclear.[40]

New nuclear power generation projects that were announced with projected costs of $2 billion are now projected to cost more than $10 billion.[41] The cost to taxpayers of just one legislative initiative to rescue these nuclear power projects could run as high as $92.8 billion. According to the Blackburn report:

A new analysis conducted for Friends of the Earth shows that tax breaks totaling $9.7 billion to $57.3 billion (depending on the type and number of reactors) would come on top of proposed subsidies totaling $35.5 billion in the Kerry-Lieberman bill. If this bill succeeds, nuclear plant owners might essentially bear no risk.[42]

Solar power has become cheaper than new nuclear power in North Carolina, and the trend is similar across the nation. Incentives that urge utilities to transition into solar power would produce better returns than similar incentives for nuclear power, due to the cost trends in the two industries.

---

[39] The plan to ship all nuclear waste to Yucca Mountain, Nevada —the only plan anywhere in the world for a comprehensive permanent repository for highly radio-active spent nuclear fuel and waste materials—, was ruled insufficient in 2004, as there has been no scientific way to demonstrate the security of the site for the projected half-life of some of the radioactive materials. Even the half-life issue is in question, as some of the materials to be stored may be significantly radioactive for up to 1,000,000 years (see EPA, Federal Register, "Public Health and Environmental Radiation Protection Standards for Yucca Mountain, Nevada; Final Rule", October 2008, ps. 61256-61287).

[40] Blackburn and Cunningham, NC WARN, July 2010, p. 7.

[41] Blackburn and Cunningham, NC WARN, July 2010, p. 8.

[42] Blackburn and Cunningham, NC WARN, July 2010, p. 12.

PORTUGAL: FROM 17% TO 45% RENEWABLE ENERGY IN 5 YEARS

Portugal is not one of the most influential players in the global energy marketplace. It also lacks a massive domestic reserve of fossil fuels to allow it to stave off dependence on foreign hydrocarbon fuels by drilling or mining domestically. It has, as a consequence, sought to drive significant expansion of clean renewable energy sources. In just five years, Portugal has expanded its renewable energy sector from 17% of national power generation to 45% this year.[43]

The International Energy Agency reported this year that "where local conditions are favourable, hydro and wind, are now fairly competitive generation technologies for baseload power generation."[44] Portugal's abundance of wind and river power has helped drive its rapid transition to what may soon be a majority clean-energy economy, uniquely insulated from economic fallout from volatility in global fossil fuel markets.

BRITISH COLUMBIA: CARBON TAX SHIFT IS WORKING

In 2008, the Canadian province of British Columbia implemented the first tax on carbon dioxide in North America. The program shifted taxation from income to carbon-based fuels, starting with a rate of $20 per ton, rising $5 per year. The second important feature of the plan is a return of revenues to taxpayers (individuals and businesses), making it a fee/dividend[45] process.

According to a report in the Victoria *Times Colonist*:

---

[43] Rosenthal, *The New York Times*, August 9, 2010.

[44] IEA, *Projected Costs of Generating Electricity: 2010 Edition*, p. 21.

[45] Citizens Climate Lobby favors a fee/dividend approach for the United States, in which 100% of revenues would be returned equally to households.

In fact, B.C.'s economic growth in 2009 — the first full year the tax was in effect — was higher than Canada's national rate. Unemployment, although high because of wider economic events, is below the national average and does not appear to have jumped when the tax shift came in.

Perhaps more significantly, for taxpayers as a whole, the carbon-tax shift has been an economic boon. During 2008 and 2009, the tax raised $846 million. However, the province tied the carbon tax to reductions in personal and corporate income taxes as well as tax credits to offset impacts on low-income individuals. The value of these offsetting cuts was nearly $1.1 billion over those two years, meaning a net tax reduction for taxpayers of about $230 million.[46]

British Columbia is taking the lead in fostering a clean energy and energy efficiency economic revolution by shifting its tax sourcing from income to carbon-intensive fuels. The carbon tax is expected to "save up to 3 million tonnes of CO_2 emissions annually — that is equal to taking almost 800,000 cars off the road each year."[47] It is expected that to achieve the target of 33% emissions reduction by 2020, a nationwide carbon tax policy would be needed. But there is clear evidence emerging from British Columbia that shifting taxation from "goods" to "bads" (from income to carbon pollution) is a spur to the local economy and is helping to build economic resilience by shifting to cleaner energy ahead of the broader economic curve.

CHINA: PLANNING TO BE GLOBAL GREEN-INDUSTRY SUPPLY LEADER

China, now the world's manufacturing leader, is on track to pass the U.S. in total energy consumption in the next decade. Even as China faces depletion of key resources and increasing dependence on imported oil, its demand for energy is

---

[46] Elgie, et al., Victoria *Times Colonist*, July 29, 2010.

[47] B.C. Government, *Carbon Tax*, July 31, 2010.

accelerating.[48] Heavily dependent on coal, China has passed the U.S. as the world leader in total CO_2 emissions. Dependence on mineral resources and fossil fuels, and consequent vulnerability to volatile global commodities markets, has led China to institute a national renewable electricity standard. To meet this standard, Beijing has pushed major investment in the manufacture and deployment of industrial-scale clean energy installations.

China now leads the world in clean energy investment, committing $34.6 billion in 2009, nearly twice U.S. investment of $18.6 billion.[49] China's investment in clean energy manufacturing is closely linked to its expansion of clean energy technology exports and clean energy generation capacity, which has reduced the cost of clean energy production for its domestic market.

As of 2009, China's total renewable energy capacity had reached 52.5 gigawatts (GW)[50], just behind the United States, which has 53.4 GW[51] of installed renewable energy capacity. Both nations cover roughly 4% of their generating capacity with renewables, but with twice the new investment in clean energy, China is on track to be the world leader in clean energy investment, manufacturing, and installed capacity, within one to two years.

Due to a lag in U.S. investment in clean energy manufacturing and installation, China has begun to move into the Texas wind market, financing the construction of a major wind complex with 625 to 648 MW of generating capacity. The project has become a vehicle for Chinese wind-turbine export to the United States. To protect its clean-energy manufacturing sector, and promote a net-export model for its clean energy economy, China requires

---

[48] IEA, 2009, p. 30.

[49] Pew, *Who's Winning the Clean Energy Race?*, p. 8.

[50] Pew, *Who's Winning the Clean Energy Race?*, p. 26.

[51] Pew, *Who's Winning the Clean Energy Race?*, p. 39.

that 70% of the components of its clean energy facilities come from Chinese domestic production.[52]

The Obama administration has responded by launching a project through the U.S. Trade and Development Agency to establish access for U.S. firms to China's clean energy market, with the aim of promoting U.S. clean energy technology exports.[53] China's early penetration into the U.S. clean energy market means the U.S. must now aim for a symbiotic export-import exchange relationship, where the U.S. will do better the more money is invested in advancing U.S. manufacturing and export of clean energy production hardware.

---

[52] Johnson, *Wall Street Journal*, October 29, 2009.

[53] USTDA, May 21, 2010.

JOB-CREATION

CARBON REDUCTION = JOB CREATION

The transition to a low-carbon economy creates the potential for a rapid and sustained expansion of jobs. Direct job creation for oil and natural gas is 0.8 jobs per $1 million in output, and coal's is 1.9 jobs per $1 million in output. Compare that to building retrofits for energy efficiency, which directly create 7 jobs per $1 million in output. Mass transit services create 11 and the smart grid creates 4.3. Wind, solar and biomass power generation, create 4.6, 5.4 and 7.4, jobs per $1 million in output respectively.

Even when adjusting for total indirect job creation potential, on the low end of energy efficiency and renewable power generation, the smart grid generates a net gain of 140.5% more job creation over and above the total direct and indirect job creation of oil and natural gas. On the high end, mass transit and biomass power generation achieve 329.7% and 235.1% more direct and indirect job creation, respectively, than oil and natural gas.[54]

According to a 2008 report conducted by the American Solar Energy Society (ASES) in Boulder, Colorado, and Management Information Services, Inc., (MISI), in Washington, DC:

We found that, in 2007, the U.S RE&EE[55] industries generated $1,045 billion in sales and created over 9 million jobs – including $10.3 billion in sales and over 91,000 jobs in Colorado. The U.S. RE&EE revenues represent substantially more than the combined 2007 sales of the three largest U.S. corporations -- Wal-Mart, ExxonMobil, and GM ($905 billion). RE&EE are growing faster than the U.S. average and contain

---

[54] Pollin, et al., *The Economic Benefits of Investing in Clean Energy*, p. 28.

[55] RE&EE = Renewable Energy and Energy Efficiency industries.

some of the most rapidly growing industries in the world, such as wind, photovoltaics, fuel cells, recycling/remanufacturing, and biofuels.[56]

The report also found that "With appropriate federal and state government policies" the renewable energy and energy efficiency sectors combined could sustain over 37 million jobs, by 2030, "including over 600,000 jobs in Colorado".[58]

The report found that gross revenues for the renewable energy (RE) industry for 2007 were "nearly $43 billion", while "the number of jobs created by RE exceeded 500,000". A disproportionate number of the jobs were scientific or in highly skilled labor, and 95% were in private industry. Biomass and biofuels accounted for roughly 70% of the total jobs created.

The ASES/MISI study also found that energy efficiency in 2007 brought in gross revenues of $1.00292 trillion in 2007, supporting an estimated 8.5866 million jobs. "More than 98 percent of the jobs were in private industry... Over 36 percent of the jobs were generated by the recycling, reuse, & remanufacturing sector."[60]

RAMPING UP INVESTMENT

According the Pew Charitable Trusts' report on *The Clean Energy Economy:*

Between 2006 and 2008, 40 states and the District of Columbia attracted venture capital investments in technologies and industries aimed at economic growth and environmental sustainability. And all states will receive a major infusion of federal funds through the recently enacted American Recovery and Reinvestment Act (ARRA), which allocates nearly $85

---

[56] ASES/MISI, p. xii.

[58] ASES/MISI, p. xii.

[60] ASES/MISI, p. xiii.

billion in direct spending and tax incentives for energy- and transportation-related programs.[61]

The Economic Benefits of Investing in Clean Energy, a report from the University of Massachusetts at Amherst Political Economy Research Institute (PERI) and the Center for American Progress, predicts a big push for renewables. The report finds that funding from the American Recovery and Reinvestment Act (ARRA) and the carbon pricing incentive of the American Clean Energy and Security Act (ACESA)[62] will complement each other and result in "an overall level of new clean-energy investments in the United States in the range of $150 billion per year over roughly the next decade."[63] Carbon tax legislation (even without a hard cap) can be expected to provide a comparable, if not stronger, incentive for investment in clean energy.[64]

That $150 billion per year of investment, mostly from the private sector, pertains only to those investments that would have a significant impact on job creation in the clean energy economy.

---

[61] Pew, *The Clean Energy Economy*, p. 4.

[62] The analysis of ACESA's role in job-creation is linked to the cost of carbon-dioxide resulting from a cap on CO_2 emissions. Direct incentives play a role in ramping up investment, but the key to emissions-reduction legislation is the contextual incentive arising from a legislative climate in which the cost of emitting carbon dioxide increases and the cost of clean renewable resources decreases. A strategy that imposes a set fee, which steadily increases over time may provide a more convincing contextual incentive for investment to move away from fossil fuels and toward clean renewables.

[63] Pollin, et al., *The Economic Benefits of Investing in Clean Energy*, p. 14.

[64] Kate Sheppard reports for Grist —3 June 2009— that the House version of cap-and-trade would aims to reduce CO_2 emissions 80% by 2050. The Carbon Tax Center estimates —see "Bills", as cited in References, below— the effect of H.R. 1337 —"America's Energy Security Trust Fund Act of 2009", introduced by Rep. Larson (D-CT) in March 2009—, which puts a steadily increasing price on carbon dioxide emissions and devotes 75% of revenues to a dividend paid directly to households, as achieving 80% reductions in CO_2 emissions by 2050.

THE 20% WIND POWER SCENARIO = 500,000 JOBS

The Department of Energy's *20% Wind Energy by 2030* report[65] conservatively estimates[66] wind power serving 20% of the national domestic energy demand by 2030. Over 500,000 jobs would be generated and "supported" under this scenario. About 180,000 of those jobs would be directly related to wind power generation, with another 320,000+ jobs spurred by new industry, including manufacturing, sales, maintenance, transmission and research.

The calculations regarding the 20 percent figure must also be treated as conservative, because wind power technology, investment and generation capacity have all expanded more rapidly than expected since 2008. What's more, the 20 percent wind energy estimate does not factor in carbon pricing, which would accelerate growth further. This is even more meaningful, when we consider that "Nationally, jobs in the clean energy economy grew by an average of 1 percent annually during the past 10 years, while total employment grew by an average of 0.4 percent annually. In 38 states and the District of Columbia, job growth in the clean energy economy outperformed total job growth between 1998 and 2007."[67]

MANUFACTURING WIND ENERGY COMPONENTS

A report from the American Wind Energy Association (AWEA) and the BlueGreen Alliance (BGA), *Winds of Change: A Manufacturing Blueprint for the Wind Industry*, looks at the job-

---

[65] DOE, *20% Wind Energy by 2030*, p. 209.

[66] DOE estimate of wind power sector serving 20% of domestic energy needs is "conservative", because it depends on a number of key assumptions, which are more conservative in terms of the pace of technological evolution than history has demonstrated—assuming for instance there are "no major innovations" in wind-power generation technology in the next 20 years.

[67] Pew, *The Clean Energy Economy*, p. 31.

creation potential for manufacturing wind power generation components:

> *Despite a weak economy, the U.S. wind energy industry broke all previous records in 2009, installing over 10,000 MW of new wind energy capacity. This incredible growth brought total installed capacity to over 35,000 MW, which is enough wind power capacity to power the equivalent of approximately 9.7 million American homes. The marked recent growth of the industry – a 39 percent average annual growth rate over the past five years – boosted the U.S. to the number one spot in 2008 for total wind energy installations, a position it maintained in 2009. The U.S. last held the title of global leader in the 1980s, when the country embraced new policies to bolster renewable forms of energy.*[68]

With the rate of growth in wind power accelerating[69], a careful redirection of energy investment incentives, at the state and federal level, can now be expected to push total wind-power generation capacity to more than 20 percent by 2030. For manufacturing, the rate of growth means:

> *Employment in manufacturing for the wind industry has grown rapidly, from 2,500 jobs in 2004 to 18,500 in 2009. There are 14,000 additional manufacturing jobs in the pipeline for wind, but these and further jobs will only come online with policies dedicated to regrowing our manufacturing sector.*[70]

---

[68] BGA, *Winds of Change*, p. 8.

[69] BGA, *Winds of Change*, p. 9: "Following the financial crisis, wind installations were expected to drop by 50 percent in 2009 – from 8,400 MW in 2008 to 4,000-5,000 MW in 2009.ı However, due to provisions in the American Recovery and Reinvestment Act of 2009 (ARRA), the wind industry was able to install over 10,000 MW of new capacity. ARRA extended the PTC through 2012, and allowed developers to convert the PTC into a 30 percent Investment Tax Credit (ITC) that could be converted into an equivalent cash grant through 2010."

[70] BGA, *Winds of Change*, p. 6.

FROM COAL JOBS TO GREEN JOBS

The coal mining industry maintains 82,595 jobs nationwide, while the wider coal industry supports 174,000 permanent jobs nationwide.[71] With conservative estimates for a transition to just 20 percent national power generation from wind showing over 500,000 jobs created, there is a clear net-gain of job-creation potential in transitioning to wind. Focusing on retooling and retraining in coal-intensive communities could secure local economies, diversify markets in coal-dependent states, and smooth the transition to clean energy in a way that expands economic growth and spreads prosperity from day one.

The AWEA/BGA report found that setting a national renewable electricity standard (RES) —a minimum percentage of total power generation from renewables— would not only motivate innovation and investment, but would create more than a quarter of a million jobs:

> *Thirty-six countries, including China and all the European Union member states, already have an RES, while in the U.S. legislation is currently pending. According to a January 2010 study by independent consulting firm Navigant Consulting, a national RES would support 274,000 additional jobs nationwide over the status quo. More than half of the direct jobs created would be in manufacturing and close to a quarter in construction.[72]*

Careful attention from legislators, in consultation with industry and affected communities, will allow the targeting of these wind-related jobs to specific areas where the coal industry is a dominant employer. In the American southwest, mining companies are already working on turning disused mining terrain into clean energy generating facilities, installing solar panels on exhausted open-pit mines in the desert. The Bagdad mine outside of Prescott, Arizona, is the proposed site for a

---

[71] SourceWatch. "Coal and Jobs in the United States".

[72] BGA, *Winds of Change*, p. 27.

15MW solar power plant, which would be the largest in the state. The Bureau of Land Management and the Environmental Protection Agency are studying the use of such lands for clean energy installations.[73]

Mining communities have great potential for clean energy production. Land values for disused mines are very low, income levels start out lower than in other regions, and there is infrastructure built in, with roads and rails already in place. In Appalachia, many of the mountainside and ridgetop coal-mining sites are no longer in use, with no prospects for future development. These sites could prove productive as wind farms, while creating real opportunity for safe, reliable, well-paid employment.

COAL RIVER MOUNTAIN: MOUNTAINTOP REMOVAL VS. WIND ENERGY

A Downstream Strategies report from December 2008 examined the cost-benefit differential for a proposed mountaintop removal project for Coal River Mountain, in Raleigh County, West Virginia. It compared the mountaintop removal project to two different scenarios involving wind energy and found that "the cumulative external costs from mountaintop removal coal production exceed the cumulative earnings in every year." Both of the wind energy scenarios studied "show cumulative earnings that exceed cumulative externalities in every year".[74]

The projected costs of negative externalities resulting from the mountaintop-removal mining scenario approach $15 million in total losses —earnings minus negative externalities— after just one year. Though there are years in which the total annual earnings for the mountaintop-removal scenario are positive, the cumulative total earnings never get to break even, when negative externalities are included. By comparison, the cumulative

---

[73] Randazzo, May 13, 2010.

[74] Hansen, et al., p. 39.

earnings, including any negative externalities, for both the conservative and the aggressive scenarios for wind power have positive cumulative earnings in every year.[75]

In terms of jobs, Hansen et al. report that:

> In the long term (five investment cycles for wind turbines), the conservative wind scenario will result in 28% more jobs than the mountaintop removal scenario. Jobs in the local industry wind scenario are 314% greater than the jobs created by mountaintop removal over five investment cycles.[76]

For the people of Raleigh County, the report showed wind energy is a more lucrative investment in terms of both job creation and public revenues. Over time, workers, communities, municipalities and the state will all earn more from the revenue stream generated by the wind scenario examined. Only landholders who benefit from favorable lease conditions and low local and state taxes would do better in the mountaintop removal scenario. Changes in laws which create this incentive would create an across-the-board incentive to shift to wind energy.

BUILDING RESILIENCE INTO LOCAL ECONOMIES

Economic resilience may be tied to ecological resilience: the sustainability of a necessary and profitable industry can be secured by the sustainability of its demand on the natural environment. The PERI/CAP report on *The Economic Benefits of Investing in Clean Energy* found that:

> Relative to spending within the fossil fuel industries, the clean energy program—including the direct spending on specific projects plus the indirect spending of purchasing supplies— utilizes far more of its overall investment budget on hiring

---

[75] Hansen, et al., p. 40.
[76] Hansen, et al., p. 35.

people, and relatively less on acquiring machines, supplies, land (either on- or offshore) and energy itself.[77]

The types of jobs created by the transition to clean, renewable resources —including the building and maintenance of the necessary advanced two-way smart-distribution infrastructure— build resilience into local economies. These jobs relate to a necessary resource for which demand tends to increase, which means they cannot be outsourced.

The same report found that the projected $150 billion in annual investment that would arise from putting a price on carbon dioxide "would generate a total of about 2.5 million jobs,"[78] adding that, "By contrast, spending the same $150 billion within the fossil-fuel industry would produce about 800,000 jobs."[79]

From 2006 to 2007, economic growth was slowing, credit tightening, and gaps beginning to show in the property market calculus that was driving economic growth, leading to the deepest recession since the Great Depression. "The real growth rate of U.S. GDP between 2006 and 2007 was 2.19%", while revenues in the U.S. renewable energy industry increased by 7.8%, when excluding hydro-electric, which reduced production.[80]

RE&EE jobs require people from all skill levels, educational backgrounds and salary grades. ASES/MISI's report suggests RE&EE will create job opportunities for the following levels of education and/or training:

---

[77] Pollin, et al., p. 31.

[78] The PERI/CAP study examines how many jobs will be created as the money is spent, not over what time precisely the jobs would be created. If the $150 billion is spent in one year, then to implement the projects it would be spent to produce, the cited number of jobs would be required to perform the work in question.

[79] Pollin, et al., p. 33.

[80] ASES/MISI, p. xiv.

- HSD/GED: e.g. solar energy system installer, wind field technician, recycling center operator;

- Apprenticeship/TS qualifications: e.g. solar systems designer, HVAC engineer, electrical system installer;

- Associate's degree: e.g. solar installation engineering technician, wind turbine technician, energy field auditor;

- Bachelor's or advanced degree: e.g. solar energy engineer, director of wind development, weatherization operations manager, energy trading specialist.

The PERI/CAP report also lists projected job creation potential for every state. Michigan, for example, could see a net gain of 53,816 jobs, while New Jersey could see a net gain of 47,519. New York could gain 109,441 new jobs, while Texas is projected to see a net gain of 152,760. Tennessee is projected to see a net gain of 39,128 jobs, while Florida could see 94,725 new jobs created. Louisiana could see a net gain of 29,095 jobs, while California could see a net employment gain of 174,927. [81]

Providing such a wide range of jobs over so wide a range of skill levels allows the RE&EE sector to empower communities economically at all levels, building long-term resilience into local and regional economies and creating a base of virtuous feedback through a more sustainable economic framework.

---

[81] Pollin, et al., p. 60.

BUILDING THE SMART GRID

CLEAN PERSISTENT RENEWABLE RESOURCES

A fundamental prerequisite for a viable future energy economy, with or without clean renewable resources, is the "smart grid", which will be able to monitor and redirect flows of electricity, while reducing leakage and improving efficiency many times over. A common complaint against wind and solar power is the concern that they are "intermittent" power sources, fluctuating with the weather and therefore inherently unreliable as a foundation for overall economic activity.

Coal is often defended as necessary for its use as a baseload power source, as is nuclear power. But baseload reliability doesn't require combustion. Renewable resources — hydroelectric, geothermal, biogas, biomass, solar thermal with storage (molten salt) and ocean thermal energy conversion— are capable of supplying reliable baseload power. An advanced two-way smart grid can deliver electricity to end users and allow for rapid realignment and redistribution of supply. By optimizing output for a consistent supply across a wider region, wind and solar voltaic power sources will gain the persistence factor of baseload power sources.

As cited above, in our review of Portugal's rapid transition to renewables, the International Energy Agency has found that "where local conditions are favourable, hydro and wind, are now fairly competitive generation technologies for baseload power generation."[82]

And in the U.S., the chairman of FERC (the Federal Energy Regulatory Commission), Jon Wellinghof, has said baseload capacity is becoming an outdated idea: "Baseload capacity really

---

[82] IEA, *Projected Costs of Generating Electricity: 2010 Edition*, p. 21.

used to only mean in an economic dispatch, which you dispatch first, what would be the cheapest thing to do. Well, ultimately wind's going to be the cheapest thing to do, so you'll dispatch that first."[83]

ENERGY & TRANSPORT MARKET DYNAMICS

Germany, the world leader in building the resources for a transition to wind and solar power, has now committed to a project that will lead the transition to a smart grid. The E-Energy project[84] is designed to speed investment to technological innovations crucial to the deployment of a national smart grid that can efficiently distribute electricity from clean energy sources. Wind and solar energy could then intelligently feed into a growing electric transport infrastructure.

E-Energy has selected 6 model regions to develop pilot projects, which will get funding from public and private sources and establish functioning regional e-energy markets by 2012. The project should establish standards for and result in the building of a smart e-energy marketplace by 2020.[85]

Building the smart electricity grid, described by some as "the internet of energy", requires training and hiring people in a range of fields at the local level. It also requires employing people on a sustained basis, over time, in localized jobs that allow no risk of outsourcing. Jobs are tied to the grid, and the grid permeates the market to which the electricity is distributed. It will be a job-creation engine.

---

[83] Straub and Behr, *Scientific American*, April 2009.

[84] "E-Energy (http://www.e-energy.de/en) is an energy supply project that will optimize Germany's energy distribution network, resulting in reduced transaction costs and increased use of RE. The German government will provide $86.9 million of the $202.7 million in total equity capital needed to mobilize the project." — Gordon, et al., *Solar Today*, June 2010.

[85] BMWi, April 2008, p. 14.

The world leader in smart-grid technology will be best positioned to capitalize on the competitive potential of clean energy sources. The smart grid opens the market for producing and exporting energy from wind, solar and geothermal. Germany controls 70% of world export market share in wind-energy technologies. An American energy economy equipped with an advanced smart grid —and so nationwide demand for renewable energy— would be positioned to compete for leadership in wind-energy technology.

U.S. CLEAN-ENERGY RESERVES EXCEED TOTAL ENERGY DEMAND

SCALING UP RENEWABLES AT 'WARTIME SPEED' IS POSSIBLE, MAY BE MOST ECONOMICALLY BENEFICIAL COURSE OF ACTION

A green economy is based on clean, renewable sources of energy that do not produce a negative impact on other areas of the economy. Building that green economy depends in large part on matching technical and commercial ingenuity with the optimal capacity of cutting-edge technologies. There is, rightly, skepticism about the potential of technologies that still represent such a small portion of energy production. But the hard data showing wind and solar can power the U.S. economy don't come from environmentalists looking through rose-colored glasses; they come from the Department of Energy and the Department of Defense.[86]

From *Plan B 3.0*, by Earth Policy Institute President Lester Brown[87]:

A worldwide survey of wind energy by the Stanford team of Cristina Archer and Mark Jacobson concluded that harnessing one fifth of the earth's available wind energy would provide seven times as much electricity as the world currently uses.

---

[86] Pew, *Reenergizing America's Defense*, 2010.

[87] From *Plan B 3.0*, by Lester R. Brown, Chapter 12, "Turning to Renewable Energy":
http://www.earth-policy.org/images/uploads/book_files/pb3ch12.pdf

[CCL NOTE: All footnotes originating in sources cited verbatim in this document are rescheduled to fit this document. Please refer to original printed or linked sources for text-specific numbering. Compound sourcing from notes extracted from source material have been left in their compound form.]

For example, China—with vast wind-swept plains in the north and west, countless mountain ridges, and a long coastline, all rich with wind—has enough readily harnessable wind energy to easily double its current electrical generating capacity.[88]

In 1991 the U.S. Department of Energy (DOE) released a national wind resource inventory, noting that three wind-rich states—North Dakota, Kansas, and Texas—had enough harnessable wind energy to satisfy national electricity needs. Advances in wind turbine design since then allow turbines to operate at lower wind speeds and to convert wind into electricity more efficiently. And because they are now 100 meters tall, instead of less than 40 meters, they harvest a far larger, stronger, and more reliable wind regime, generating 20 times as much electricity as the turbines installed in the early 1980s when modern wind power development began. With these new turbine technologies, the three states singled out by DOE could satisfy not only national electricity needs but national energy needs.[89]

In addition, a 2005 DOE assessment of offshore wind energy concluded that U.S. offshore wind out to a distance of 50 miles alone is sufficient to meet 70 percent of national electricity needs. Europe is already tapping its offshore wind. A 2004 assessment by the Garrad Hassan wind energy consulting group concluded that if governments aggressively develop their

---

[88] Cristina L. Archer and Mark Z. Jacobson, "Evaluation of Global Windpower," *Journal of Geophysical Research*, vol. 110 (30 June 2005); Jean Hu et al., "Wind: The Future is Now," *Renewable Energy World*, July–August 2005, p. 212.

[89] D. L. Elliott, L. L. Wendell, and G. L. Gower, *An Assessment of the Available Windy Land Area and Wind Energy Potential in the Contiguous United States* (Richland, WA: Pacific Northwest Laboratory, 1991); C. L. Archer and M. Z. Jacobson, "The Spatial and Temporal Distributions of U.S. Winds and Wind Power at 80m Derived from Measurements," *Journal of Geophysical Research*, 16 May 2003.

vast offshore resources, wind could supply all of Europe's residential electricity by 2020.[90]

The United States could lead a global design and manufacturing revolution in the production of clean energy technology and infrastructure. To do this, market conditions —i.e. putting a price on carbon— must be adjusted to create the incentive for private-sector investment to flow toward those technologies.

SOLAR ENERGY RESERVES

The amount of solar energy striking the Earth far exceeds the amount of energy required for power generation. Even in northern Maine, the Department of Energy estimates four to five kWh per square meter per day. In the rainy coastal regions of Washington state, estimates are still as high as three to four kWh per m^2 per day.[91]

Total annual U.S. domestic energy consumption is calculated by the Department of Energy in Btu (1 kWh is equal to 3,412.1416 Btu). The total U.S. domestic energy consumption for 2008 is reported as 100.1 quadrillion Btu.[92] The United States has a total land area[93] of 9,161,966 km² or 9.161966 trillion m². If we set the national average solar intensity at the low end, just 3 kWh per day per m², the total amount of solar energy striking the United States is 27.485898 trillion kWh per day or 10.0323528 quadrillion kWh per year, more than 342 times total U.S. demand.

---

[90] W. Musial and S. Butterfield, *Future of Offshore Wind Energy in the United States* (Golden, CO: DOE, National Renewable Energy Laboratory (NREL), June 2004); U.S. electricity consumption from DOE, EIA, Electric Power Annual 2005 (Washington, DC: November 2006); Garrad Hassan and Partners, Sea Wind Europe (London: Greenpeace, March 2004).

[91] NREL, *Average Daily Solar Radiation per Month.*

[92] EIA, *Annual Energy Outlook 2010*, p. 87.

[93] Land area figure quoted from the CIA publication *The World Factbook.*

CUTTING-EDGE EFFICIENCY GAINS
(TECHNOLOGIES ON THE HORIZON)

There are cutting-edge innovations that, while not ready to be included in the standard renewable energy portfolio, have the potential to greatly expand our capacity to produce clean energy. Policies that put a clear price on carbon-intensive fuels —as seen in Germany or British Columbia— drive investment to breakthrough technologies, speeding their development and deployment.

A glimpse at some of the possibilities:

High-altitude tethered wind turbines: If deployed, these would harvest persistent wind energy from the jet stream, at 15,000 to 30,000 feet, an altitude where just 1% of available wind energy is enough to power global energy needs.[94]

Helium kite turbines: At lower altitudes, highly mobile helium kite turbines[95], such as the air rotor system (MARS) developed by Magenn Power[96], allow for rapid deployment of mobile, localized "wind power anywhere" electricity generation systems, to remote, poor communities with no access to an electric grid. This technology could revolutionize emergency response, rescue and security operations and community development in remote areas.

Vertical axis wind turbines (VAWT): Utilizing MagLev (magnetic levitation), engineers are working on a VAWT that would produce 1 gigawatt of electricity from a single turbine, enough to power 750,000 homes. It would take 1,000 conventional wind turbines to power 500,000 homes. The MagLev VAWT[97] would require less

---

[94] Levesque, July 17, 2007.

[95] LaMonica, January 4, 2007.

[96] http://www.magenn.com/products.php

[97] Basantani, November 26, 2007.

than 100 acres, as compared to a field of 1,000 conventional wind turbines, which would be spread out over 64,000 acres.[98]

Organic solar concentrators (OSC): These photo-voltaic (PV) cells, mounted along the inside edge of specially designed windows,[99] hold great promise for retrofitting buildings of all kinds, from any period, to harvest clean electricity from sunlight. Being embedded into windows, they can greatly expand the available surface area for retrofitting old structures for solar power generation.

Photo-voltaic "Glitter": The powerful PV "glitter"[100] technology, developed at Sandia National Labs, is capable of 100 times the silicon-to-energy efficiency of traditional solar cells. It can be infused into fabrics, building materials and plastics, to achieve revolutionary expansion of the solar-capable smart grid, while reducing the need for batteries and for wall-charging of electronics.

Launched July 2010:[101] Molten salt solar-thermal plants[102] allow for "de-coupling the collection of solar energy from producing power", including nighttime storage of solar-thermal energy, for release to the grid during peak evening hours or inclement weather, an important expansion of the potential of solar power. According to Sandia National Labs, the solar thermal energy can be stored in molten salt for up to a week, and "two-tank storage system [one hot salt storage tank and one cold salt storage tank] could have an annual efficiency of about 99 percent".

---

[98] While most of the land across which a 1,000-turbine wind-farm would be distributed would be available for other uses, the limited availability of such continuous spaces for uniform development makes the single VAWT model an attractive alternative in some regions, and a way of expanding the investment potential, or capital draw, of wind energy.

[99] Currie, et al., 11 July 2008.

[100] Sandia National Labs, December 21, 2009.

[101] Falasca, *GreenMe.it*, 14 July 2010.

[102] Sandia National Labs, January 10, 2006.

CLEAN ENERGY & THE NATIONAL DEFENSE

THE SECURITY ENVIRONMENT

The Department of Defense has also adopted an energy security strategy based on diversification into clean renewable energy sources, recognizing the destabilization of global climate patterns as a major threat to international peace and security.[103] The *Quadrennial Defense Review Report,* published in February, found that "climate change will shape the operating environment, roles, and missions that we undertake", and that "climate-related changes are already being observed in every

---

[103] A report from the Center for Naval Analyses (CNA) —funded by Defense funds for the explicit purpose of shaping Pentagon policy— published in May 2009, specifically examines "The National Security Threats of America's Current Energy Posture", finding that:

> "America's current energy posture has resulted in the following national security risks: • U.S. dependence on oil weakens international leverage, undermines foreign policy objectives, and entangles America with unstable or hostile regimes. • Inefficient use and overreliance on oil burdens the military, undermines combat effectiveness, and exacts a huge price tag—in dollars and lives. • U.S. dependence on fossil fuels undermines economic stability, which is critical to national security. • A fragile domestic electricity grid makes our domestic military installations, and their critical infrastructure, unnecessarily vulnerable to incident, whether deliberate or accidental." (CNA, p. 1.)

CNA's Military Advisory Board specifically warned that "The nation's current energy posture is a serious and urgent threat to national security" (41), "A business as usual approach to energy security poses an unacceptably high threat level from a series of converging risks" (42), and "inefficient use of energy can create serious vulnerabilities to our forces at multiple levels" (45).

Recommendations for resolving this "unacceptably high threat level" relating to energy insecurity include: "wide-scale adoption of distributed and renewable energy generation" (48), as part of a broad-spectrum "new energy paradigm" (49).

region of the world".[104] The Pentagon report also observes that fallout from climate destabilization will lead to food and water shortages, mass migration and potentially the breakdown of political institutions around the world.[105]

The European Union's experience with fossil-fuel dependence helps to illustrate the subtle ways in which a shortfall in clean energy production capacity can jeopardize security interests. As Europe's dependence on imported natural gas for domestic energy and heating deepens, key U.S. allies become vulnerable to political manipulations from abroad, which erodes American diplomatic power and influence. A report in the Spring 2010 edition of the *Columbia University Journal of Politics and Society* finds that:

> *This dependence, in conjunction with an EU energy market that remains divided along national borders and a pattern of bilateral deals between European national energy monopolies and external suppliers endangers not only cooperation within Europe but also the reliability and independence of European diplomatic and political action with regards to U.S. interests (Noël 2008, 8).[106]*

This crisis of fossil-fuel dependence stems in part from the fragmentation of Europe's energy distribution infrastructure and import markets, which has put E.U. member states at risk of market manipulation by large external suppliers like Russian gas giant Gazprom. A multi-resource-capable smart grid would reduce the power that suppliers have to dictate market conditions. Such a system "would allow for easier substitution of energy sources, a critical step for integrating renewable technologies undergoing expansion in both Europe and the United States."[107]

---

[104] QDR, February 2010, p. 84.

[105] QDR, February 2010, p. 85.

[106] Stetsenko, p. 71.

[107] Stetsenko, p. 83.

Renewables are a necessary component of integrated diversification. Sustainable economic recovery also depends on deploying credit and investment in a way that empowers small businesses and communities to engage the clean energy revolution with a wave of long-term job creation.[108]

Diversification of domestic energy economies into a wide range of clean renewable technologies is not just an ecological imperative, but an economic and political security imperative. Dependence on foreign suppliers of hydrocarbon-based energy erodes national sovereignty and undermines economic and political security. Pioneering the technology to build that new energy economy will have long-term benefits for both security and economic wellbeing.

PUBLIC-PRIVATE PARTNERSHIPS, PIONEERING R&D

In 2006, the Worldwatch Institute reported on research funded by DoD to explore ways to increase the productivity of solar energy harvesting technology, using semiconducting nanoparticles. Starting in 2004:

> *the U.S. Department of Defense granted over $18 million to three nanotech start-up companies to develop military applications of solar energy. With additional backing from corporate partners and venture capitalists, Nanosys (Palo Alto, California), NanoSolar (also in Palo Alto), and Konarka (Lowell, Massachusetts) are developing a new generation of lightweight, flexible solar cells that are based on semiconducting nanoparticles. Inorganic nanomaterials such as quantum dots that absorb a wide spectrum of light are printed on large sheets of metal foil that can be rolled out like plastic wrap onto rooftops—allowing homes or office buildings*

---

[108] See our JOB-CREATION section, for more information on the specifics of how wind power and other carbon-free power-generation methods are already creating jobs and hold promise for long-term economic growth and resilience.

to generate their own power. NanoSolar is also developing a semiconductor paint that could allow nano-powered solar cells to be applied to any surface.[109]

By the time the Worldwatch Institute had published its 2006 report, National Geographic had reported the following:

Like paint, the composite can be sprayed onto other materials and used as portable electricity. A sweater coated in the material could power a cell phone or other wireless devices. A hydrogen-powered car painted with the film could potentially convert enough energy into electricity to continually recharge the car's battery.

The researchers envision that one day "solar farms" consisting of the plastic material could be rolled across deserts to generate enough clean energy to supply the entire planet's power needs.[110]

Now, the Norwegian firm EnSol has developed a sprayable solar paint, which is expected to be available to the wider consumer market by 2016. The spray would allow any surface —a window, a wall— to be transformed into a device capable of converting up to 20 percent of the solar power striking the surface to electricity.[111] NextGen Solar has reportedly produced a solar paint that "is expected to provide up to 40% efficiency at a third of the cost of traditional photovoltaic panels."[112] There is a race among commercial and non-commercial entities pursuing research on solar paint technologies that could revolutionize the entire energy and fuel economy within the decade.[113]

---

[109] Shand and Wetter, p. 87.

[110] Lovgren, *National Geographic*, January 14, 2005.

[111] Scott, *Inhabitat*, August 10, 2010.

[112] Schwartz, *Inhabitat*, April 12, 2010.

[113] Not only are the firms NanoSolar, Nanosys and Konarka, continuing the research the Pentagon funded in 2004, with EnSol and NextGen Solar racing to produce the first commercially viable paint-on solar film, but researchers at the University of Texas, the National Institute of

Such cutting-edge research is ongoing, but constitutes only one facet of the DoD alternative fuels strategy. Planning is underway to transition military installations large and small from a net-import power standard to a net-zero power standard. Utilizing a wide array of renewable and locally distributed power-generation resources, along with an electrified vehicle fleet, a larger number of military installations would become self-sufficient in terms of power generation.

DEPARTMENT OF DEFENSE: DEPLOYING CLEAN ENERGY TECHNOLOGIES

The U.S. Army has begun installing state of the art wind turbines on its bases, and is exploring ways to improve energy efficiency. By deploying electric vehicles and scaling up use of solar power-generation, the Army hopes to achieve the goal of operational energy independence. Private industry can benefit from the efficiency gains achieved through the military R&D process and by providing parts and services to the military to carry out this transition.

The U.S. Air Force is "one of the nation's largest purchasers of environmentally friendly energy sources such as biomass, wind, landfill gas, and solar energy." The Air Force is also aggressively pursuing energy conservation and energy efficiency, resulting in savings that run into the billions of dollars.[114]

The U.S. Navy has commissioned what it says is the first in a new fleet of "green ships." The U.S.S. Makin Island:

> *is the final amphibious assault ship built in the LHD-1 Wasp-class, but is the first of the class built with gas turbine engines and electric drive. The Navy projects that this advance will*

Standards and Technology, and the National Renewable Energy Laboratory, are also working on similar products.

[114] Billings, "Sustaining the mission through green innovation", 2009.

save nearly $250 million in fuel costs over the ship's lifetime.[115]

Such innovations save money and reduce vulnerability to cost shocks in the fossil fuels markets. They also reduce overall carbon emissions and enable the deployment of new low-emissions vehicles and clean-energy military installations.

---

[115] Surface Forces Public Affairs, "'Green Ship' USS Makin Island Brought to Life in San Diego", 2009.

CONCLUSIONS

CLEAN ENERGY & EMISSIONS REDUCTION ARE A NATIONAL IMPERATIVE.

A transition toward a clean-energy economy, resulting in CO_2 levels of 350 ppm or less, is a national imperative. Our economy, environment and security depend on it. The transition will require investment, but all costs need not be borne by the U.S. government or households and consumers. Studies cited show a commitment in both form (legislation) and function (incentives, standards, goals) from government can shift investment priorities in the private sector.

CARBON PRICING IS AN ENGINE FOR MAJOR PRIVATE INVESTMENT.

Germany's success in spurring private-sector investments through effective public policy has made it the world leader in exporting clean energy technology. Some of its leading industrial and financial firms are now world-leading stakeholders in the clean energy future. It is estimated that provisions of the American Recovery and Reinvestment Act, coupled with legislation that puts a price on carbon dioxide emissions, would lead to $150 billion per year in mostly private investments, over the next decade, creating millions of new jobs.

RENEWABLES WILL OUT-COMPETE FOSSIL FUELS WITH POLICY SHIFT.

Conventional wisdom holds that renewable resources like wind and solar are "intermittent" and do not have the capacity to meet current energy demand. This is true insofar as the current infrastructure is not sufficient to meet active demand with clean energy. However, the potential for expansion of existing clean energy technologies is sufficient to cover energy needs if a sufficiently smart power grid is deployed to correct for localized fluctuations in wind flow or solar intensity. Putting a price on carbon dioxide emissions can steer investment to energy sources like wind and solar that are more sustainable, economical and environmentally healthy.

REGIONAL DISPARITIES IN CARBON TAX IMPACT ARE MINIMAL.

The American Enterprise Institute has found that regional disparities in the economic impact —primarily energy costs— resulting from a carbon tax are "sufficiently small that one could argue that a carbon tax is distributionally neutral across regions."[119] Wider disparities can be minimized with targeted dividend adjustments and other incentives.[120]

CLEAN ENERGY & ENERGY EFFICIENCY = MASSIVE JOB CREATION.

Job creation resulting from a transition to a zero-combustion transport economy and clean rewewable energy resources, along with industries that foster energy efficiency, have the potential to create millions of new jobs essential to the resulting economic landscape, jobs that could not be outsourced.

---

[119] Hassett, et al., p. 3.

[120] Resources for the Future reports that regional disparities could reach as high as 2% of total annual income, but planning with regard to how dividends are paid from a carbon pricing plan can reduce that disparity. In later years, a steadily increasing fee, coupled with a 100% uniform dividend, could also potentially cover such a disparity.

RURAL & COAL-INTENSIVE COMMUNITIES WILL BENEFIT.

Rural communities, and communities tied to the coal industry will experience an injection of new capital and the expansion of new economic opportunity. The job market in rural and coal-intensive communities will not only expand, but will see income levels rise, if the right investments are made for developing clean energy resources. Major impacts to human and environmental health related to coal will be reduced and/or eliminated. The very same companies that presently depend on mining or burning coal for their revenues can benefit from diversifying into a broad-spectrum clean energy portfolio.

U.S. COULD LEAD A GLOBAL CLEAN ENERGY ECONOMY.

The United States enjoys a unique geographical wealth in terms of clean energy resources, with some of the most abundant reserves of easily accessible wind, solar and geothermal energy. It could, with astute policy planning, take the global lead both in clean energy production and in manufacturing and exporting clean energy technology. The United States military is actively participating in the clean-energy transition, with major investments in R&D, retrofitting and efficiency, and could be a testing-ground for consumer-level technologies.

SUSTAINABLE ENERGY POLICY IS A MATTER OF NATIONAL SECURITY.

"A business as usual approach to energy security poses an unacceptably high threat level from a series of converging risks."[121] Competition among leading regional and minerals markets —China, E.U., Russian Federation, OPEC, North America— means the rapidly expanding demand for combustible

---

[121] CNA, 2009, p. ix.

fuels is a threat to agriculture and the security of the world food supply. Diplomatic independence requires energy independence, which in turn requires distributed, localized clean renewable resources, an advanced smart grid, and the new enterprises that come with building and managing this new paradigm.

LEADING NOW COSTS LESS THAN CATCHING UP LATER.

The costs inherent in building a clean energy economy now will ultimately be far lower, given the negative externalities — including environmental, economic and political security risks—inherent in not moving away from carbon-based fuels. Whether one accepts or rejects projections about mounting, compounded fallout from global climate destabilization, a wide array of security-related and economic costs can be mitigated or averted by moving ahead with the clean energy transition now. Using carbon-pricing policy to motivate this transition is the most responsible economic response. It will create jobs and provide clarity of cost-projection for businesses and investors.

REFERENCES

1.   American Solar Energy Society (ASES); Management Information Services, Inc. (MISI). *Defining, Estimating, and Forecasting the Renewable Energy and Energy Efficiency Industries in the U.S. and in Colorado.* December 2008. URL: http://www.ases.org/images/stories/ASES/pdfs/CO_Jobs_Final_Report_December2008.pdf

2.   Archer, Cristina L.; Jacobson, Mark Z. "Evaluation of Global Windpower," *Journal of Geophysical Research,* vol. 110, 30 June 2005. URL: http://www.agu.org/pubs/crossref/2005/2004JD005462.shtml

3.   Archer, Cristina L.; Jacobson, Mark Z. "The Spatial and Temporal Distributions of U.S. Winds and Wind Power at 80m Derived from Measurements," *Journal of Geophysical Research,* 16 May 2003. URL: http://www.agu.org/pubs/crossref/2003/2002JD002076.shtml

4.   Basantani, Mahesh. "The MagLev: The Super-powered Magnetic Wind Turbine". *Inhabitat.* November 26, 2007. URL: http://www.inhabitat.com/2007/11/26/super-powered-magnetic-wind-turbine-maglev/

5.   B.C. Government. *Carbon Tax.* British Columbia, as viewed July 31, 2010. URL: http://www.gov.bc.ca/yourbc/carbon_tax/ct_planet.html?src=/planet/ct_planet.html

6.   BGA. *Winds of Change: A Manufacturing Blueprint for the Wind Industry.* American Wind Energy Association; BlueGreen Alliance (BGA); United Steel Workers. URL: http://www.awea.org/documents/BGA_Report_062510_FINAL.pdf?id=0050

7.   Billings, Kevin, W. "Sustaining the mission through green innovation". U.S. Air Force. April 21, 2009. URL: http://www.af.mil/news/story.asp?id=123145452

8. Blackburn, John O.; Cunningham, Sam; NC WARN. *Solar and Nuclear Costs — The Historic Crossover: Solar Energy is Now the Better Buy*. North Carolina Waste Awareness & Reduction Network. Durham, NC. July 2010.

9. BMWi (German Federal Ministry of Economics and Technology). *E-Energy: ICT-based Energy System of the Future*. Munich, April 2008. URL: http://www.e-energy.de/documents/Brochure_E-Energy_300608.pdf

10. Boselli, Muriel. "Green energy investment surviving crisis, says IEA". Reuters. London. May 27, 2010. URL: http://www.reuters.com/article/idUSTRE64Q4D920100527

11. Boumedjout, Hichem. "Morocco hopes to shine in mega solar project". Science and Development Network. Algiers, 20 January 2010. URL: http://www.scidev.net/en/news/morocco-hopes-to-shine-in-mega-solar-project.html

12. Brown, Lester R. *Plan B 3.0: Mobilizing to Save Civilization*. Earth Policy Institute. W.W. Norton & Company, New York. 2008. URL: http://www.earth-policy.org/index.php?/books/pb3

13. Brown, Lester R. *Plan B 4.0: Mobilizing to Save Civilization*. Earth Policy Institute. W.W. Norton & Company, New York. 2009. URL: http://www.earthpolicy.org/index.php?/books/pb4

14. Bureau of Labor Statistics. "News Release: The Employment Situation — August 2010". U.S. Department of Labor, Washington, DC. September 3, 2010. URL: http://www.bls.gov/news.release/pdf/empsit.pdf

15. Burnett, John. "Winds of Change Blow into Roscoe, Texas". *All Things Considered*. NPR. November 27, 2007. URL: http://www.npr.org/templates/story/story.php?storyId=16658695

16. Burtraw, Dallas; Sweeney, Richard; Walls, Margaret. *The Incidence of U.S. Climate Policy: Alternative Uses of Revenues from a Cap-and-Trade Auction*. Resources for the Future. Washington, DC. May 22, 2009. URL: http://www.rff.org/RFF/Documents/RFF-DP-09-17.pdf

17. Carbon Tax Center. "Bills". May 12, 2010. New York. URL: http://www.carbontax.org/progress/carbon-tax-bills/

18. Carbon Tax Center. "Regional Disparities". April 26, 2010. New York. URL: http://www.carbontax.org/issues/regional-disparities/

19. CIA. "United States". *The World Factbook*. As updated August 19, 2010. URL: https://www.cia.gov/library/publications/the-world-factbook/geos/us.html

20. CNA. *Powering America's Defense: Energy and the Risks to National Security*. Alexandria, VA. May 2009. URL: http://www.cna.org/sites/default/files/Powering%20Americas%20Defense.pdf

21. Currie, Michael J.; Mapel, Jonathan K.; Heidel, Timothy D.; Goffri, Shalom; Baldo, Marc A. "High-Efficiency Organic Solar Concentrators for Photovoltaics". *Science*, Vol. 321. no. 5886. 11 July 2008. Ps. 226-228. URL: http://www.sciencemag.org/cgi/content/short/321/5886/226

22. Department of Energy. *20% Wind Energy by 2030: Increasing Wind Energy's Contribution to U.S. Electricity Supply*. July 2008. URL: http://www.20percentwind.org/20percent_wind_energy_report_revOct08.pdf

23. Department of Energy. *Electric Power Annual 2005*. Washington, DC, November 2006. URL: http://tonto.eia.doe.gov/ftproot/electricity/034805.pdf

24. Desertec Foundation. *Clean Power from Deserts: The DESERTEC Concept for Energy, Water and Climate Security*. WhiteBook, 4th edition. Bonn, February 2009. URL: http://www.desertec.org/fileadmin/downloads/DESERTEC-WhiteBook_en_small.pdf

25. EIA. *Annual Energy Outlook 2010*. U.S. Energy Information Administration. Washington, DC, April 2010. URL: http://www.eia.doe.gov/oiaf/aeo/pdf/0383(2010).pdf

26. Eilperin, Juliet. "New Plan Ordered For Yucca Mountain: Court Seeks Extended Radiation Guards". *Washington Post*. July 10, 2004. " URL: http://www.washingtonpost.com/wp-dyn/articles/A38751-2004Jul9.html

27. Elgie, Stewart; Rivers, Nic; Olewiler, Nancy. "B.C.'s carbon tax is looking like a winner: Experts agree that the measure is working. Is anyone else watching?" Victoria *Times Colonist*. Victoria, British Columbia, 29 July 2010. URL: http://www.timescolonist.com/technology/carbon+looking+like+winner/3335477/story.html

28. Elliott, D.L.; Wendell, L.L.; and Gower, G.L. *An Assessment of the Available Windy Land Area and Wind Energy Potential in the Contiguous United States*. Pacific Northwest Laboratory. Richland, WA, 1991. URL: http://www.osti.gov/energycitations/product.biblio.jsp?osti_id=525 2760

29. EPA. "Public Health and Environmental Radiation Protection Standards for Yucca Mountain, Nevada; Final Rule." Federal Register Vol. 73, No. 200 (15 October 2008): 61256-61289. URL: http://www.epa.gov/radiation/docs/yucca/yucca_mtn_rule_fed_reg _version.pdf

30. Falasca, Simona. "Enel inaugura in Sicilia Archimede, la centrale solare termodinamica che funziona anche di notte". *GreenMe.it*. 14 July 2010. URL: http://www.greenme.it/informarsi/energie-rinnovabili/2734-enel-inaugura-in-sicilia-archimede-la-centrale-solare-termodinamica-che-funziona-anche-di-notte

31. Garrad Hassan and Partners, Ltd. *Sea Wind Europe*. Greenpeace. London, March 2004. URL: http://www.greenpeace.org.uk/files/pdfs/migrated/MultimediaFiles /Live/FullReport/6230.pdf

32. Gordon, Kate; Wong, Julian L.; McLain, J.T. "Out of the Running?" *Solar Today*. Vol. 24, No. 5. June 2010. URL: http://www.solartoday-digital.org/solartoday/201006#pg1

33. Gray, Tom. "Wind Factory Watch: Eagle Claw, Oklahoma". *Into the Wind*. AWEA. June 30, 2010. URL: http://www.awea.org/blog/index.php?mode=viewid&post_id=410

34. Hansen, Evan; Collins, Alan; Hendryx, Michael; Boettner, Fritz; Hereford, Anne. *The Long-term Economics Benefits of Wind Versus Mountaintop Removal Coal on Coal River Mountain, West Virginia*. Downstream Strategies. Morgantown, WV. December 2008. URL: http://www.downstreamstrategies.com/Documents/reports_publica tion/Wind_vs_mountaintop_removal_coal_Coal_River_Mtn_Dec2008. pdf

35. Hassett, Kevin A.; Mathur, Aparna; Metcalf, Gilbert E. *The Incidence of a U.S. Carbon Tax: A Lifetime and Regional Analysis*. American Enterprise Institute for Public Policy Research. January 2008. URL: http://www.aei.org/docLib/20080201_USCarbonTax.pdf

36. Hu, Jean, et al., "Wind: The Future is Now," *Renewable Energy World*, July–August 2005.

37. International Energy Agency. *Key World Energy Statistics.* Paris, 2009. URL: http://www.iea.org/statistics/

38. International Energy Agency. *Projected Costs of Generating Electricity: 2010 Edition.* Paris, March 2010. Full report purchase URL: http://iea.org/w/bookshop/add.aspx?id=403 / Executive Summary (ps. 17-25) URL: http://www.iea.org/Textbase/npsum/ElecCost2010SUM.pdf

39. Johnson, Keith. "Lone Star, Meet Red Star: China's $1.5 Billion Wind-Power Deal in Texas". *Wall Street Journal.* October 29, 2009. URL: http://blogs.wsj.com/environmentalcapital/2009/10/29/lone-star-meet-red-star-chinas-15-billion-wind-power-deal-in-texas/

40. Knigge, Markus; Görlach, Benjamin. *Effects of Germany's Ecological Tax Reforms on the Environment, Employment and Technological Innovation* (Summary of the Final Report of the Project: „Quantifizierung der Effekte der Ökologischen Steuerreform auf Umwelt, Beschäftigung und Innovation"). Research Project commissioned by the German Federal Environmental Agency (UBA). August 2005. URL: http://www.umweltbundesamt.de/uba-info-presse-e/hintergrund/oekosteuer.pdf

41. LaMonica, Martin. "Going aloft for wind power". *CNET News.* January 4, 2007. URL: http://news.cnet.com/Going-aloft-for-wind-power/2100-1008_3-6147225.html

42. Levesque, Tylene. "Flying Wind Turbines". *Inhabitat.* July 17, 2007. URL: http://www.inhabitat.com/2007/07/17/flying-wind-turbines/

43. Lovgren, Stefan. "Spray-On Solar-Power Cells are True Breakthrough". National Geographic News. January 14, 2005. URL: http://news.nationalgeographic.com/news/2005/01/0114_050114_solarplastic.html

44. McIlmoil, Rory; Hansen, Evan; Boettner, Ted. *Coal and Renewables in Central Appalachia: The Impact of Coal on the Tennessee State Budget.* June 22, 2010. URL: http://www.downstreamstrategies.com/Documents/reports_publication/DownstreamStrategies-coalTN.pdf

45. McIlmoil, Rory; Hansen, Evan; Boettner, Ted; Miller, Paul. *Coal and Renewables in Central Appalachia: The Impact of Coal on the West Virginia State Budget*. June 22, 2010. URL: http://www.downstreamstrategies.com/Documents/reports_publica tion/DownstreamStrategies-coalWV.pdf

46. Musial, W.; Butterfield, S. *Future of Offshore Wind Energy in the United States*. National Renewable Energy Laboratory (NREL), Department of Energy. Golden, CO, June 2004. URL: http://www.nrel.gov/docs/fy04osti/36313.pdf

47. NJCEP. "New Jersey Solar Installations by Year As of 7/31/10". State of New Jersey Board of Public Utilities. August 2010. URL: http://www.njcleanenergy.com/files/file/Renewable_Programs/CG %20Updates%20/NJ_Solar_Installations_as_of_073110.xls

48. NJCEP. "Renewable Energy Incentive Program Incentives". State of New Jersey Board of Public Utilities. As viewed 4 September 2010. URL: http://www.njcleanenergy.com/re

49. NREL. *Average Daily Solar Radiation per Month*. U.S. Department of Energy. URL: http://www.energysavers.gov/pdfs/208.pdf

50. NREL. *Estimates of Windy1 Land Area and Wind Energy Potential by State for Areas >= 30% Capacity Factor at 80m*. U.S. Department of Energy. February 4, 2010. URL: http://www.windpoweringamerica.gov/pdfs/wind_maps/wind_pote ntial.pdf

51. Pew Charitable Trusts. *The Clean Energy Economy: Repowering Jobs, Businesses and Investments Across America*. June 2009. URL: http://www.pewcenteronthestates.org/uploadedFiles/Clean_Econo my_Report_Web.pdf

52. Pew Charitable Trusts. *Who's Winning the Clean Energy Race? Growth, Competition and Opportunity in the World's Largest Economies: G-20 Clean Energy Factbook*. March 2010. URL: http://www.pewtrusts.org/uploadedFiles/wwwpewtrustsorg/Report s/Global_warming/G-20%20Report.pdf?n=5939

53. Pew Project on National Security, Energy and Climate. *Reenergizing America's Defense: How the Armed Forces Are Stepping Forward to Combat Climate Change and Improve the U.S. Energy Posture*. 2010: URL: http://www.pewclimatesecurity.org/reenergizing-americas-defense/

54. Pollin, Robert; Heintz, James; Garrett-Peltier, Heidi. *The Economic Benefits of Investing in Clean Energy: How the economic stimulus program and new legislation can boost U.S. economic growth and employment.* Department of Economics and Political Economy Research Institute (PERI), University of Massachusetts, Amherst; Center for American Progress. June 2009. URL: http://www.americanprogress.org/issues/2009/06/clean_energy.html

55. Quadrennial Defense Review. *Quadrennial Defense Review Report.* U.S. Department of Defense, Washington, DC. February 2010. URL: http://www.defense.gov/QDR/images/QDR_as_of_12Feb10_1000.pdf

56. Randazzo, Ryan. "Are mine sites the future of solar? Experts: Such land could cut costs of building sun plants" *The Arizona Republic.* May 13, 2010. URL: http://www.azcentral.com/arizonarepublic/business/articles/2010/05/13/20100513biz-solarmines0513.html

57. Reuters. "E.ON takes first step into U.S. renewables market". October 4, 2007. URL: http://www.reuters.com/article/idUSWEB838020071005

58. Reuters. "Munich Re touts Sahara in solar energy push". June 16, 2009. URL: http://www.reuters.com/article/idUSLG48059620090616

59. Rosenthal, Elisabeth. "Beyond Fossil Fuels: Portugal Gives Itself a Clean-Energy Makeover". *The New York Times.* August 9, 2010. URL: http://www.nytimes.com/2010/08/10/science/earth/10portugal.html?_r=1

60. Sandia National Labs. "Advantages of Using Molten Salt". National Solar Thermal Test Facility. Albuquerque, NM, January 10, 2006. URL: http://www.sandia.gov/Renewable_Energy/solarthermal/NSTTF/salt.htm

61. Sandia National Labs. "Glitter-sized solar photovoltaics produce competitive results: Adventures in microsolar supported by microelectronics and MEMS techniques". Albuquerque, NM, December 21, 2009. URL: https://share.sandia.gov/news/resources/news_releases/glitter-sized-solar-photovoltaics-produce-competitive-results/

62. Schwartz, Ariel. "NextGen Announces Cheap Solar Paint on the Horizon". *Inhabitat.* April 12, 2010. URL: http://inhabitat.com/2010/04/12/nextgen-announces-cheap-solar-paint-on-the-horizon/

63. Scott, Cameron. "Transparent Solar Spray Transforms Windows Into Watts". *Inhabitat.* August 10, 2010. URL: http://inhabitat.com/2010/08/10/transparent-solar-spray-transforms-windows-into-watts/

64. Shand, Hope; Wetter, Kathy Jo. "Shrinking Science: An Introduction to Nanotechnology". *State of the World 2006.* The Worldwatch Institute. Ps. 78-95. URL: http://www.worldwatch.org/node/3996

65. Sheppard, Kate. "Everything you always wanted to know about the Waxman-Markey energy/climate bill—in bullet points". *Grist.* 3 June 2009. URL: http://www.grist.org/article/2009-06-03-waxman-markey-bill-breakdown/

66. Smith, Rebecca; Gold, Russell. "New Jersey Outshines 48 of Its Peers in Solar Power: Lacking California's Sunshine and Deserts, State Capitalizes on Utility Poles and Flat Industrial Roofs to Claim No. 2 Spot". *Wall Street Journal.* July 31, 2009. URL: http://online.wsj.com/article/SB124900300175395743.html

67. SourceWatch. "Coal and Jobs in the United States". URL: http://www.sourcewatch.org/index.php?title=Coal_and_jobs_in_the_United_States

68. Sroka-Holzmann, Pamela. "PSE&G installing solar panels in Hillsborough". *Courier News & Home News Tribune.* Hillsborough, NJ, July 27, 2010. URL: http://www.mycentraljersey.com/article/20100727/NEWS/7270330/PSE-G-installing-solar-panels-in-Hillsborough

69. Stetsenko, Andrei. "Cooperation and Integration: Recommendations for Transatlantic Energy Security". *Columbia University Journal of Politics & Society.* Volume XXI, Spring 2010. The Helvidius Group of Columbia University New York. Ps. 71-102. URL: http://www.helvidius.org/index.php?page=post&article_id=5

70. Straub, Noelle; Behr, Peter. "Will the U.S. Ever Need to Build Another Coal or Nuclear Power Plant? The new chairman of the Federal Energy Regulatory Commission doesn't think so". *Scientific American.* April 22, 2009. URL:

http://www.scientificamerican.com/article.cfm?id=will-the-us-need-new-coal

71. Surface Forces Public Affairs. "'Green Ship' USS Makin Island Brought to Life in San Diego". U.S. Navy. October 26, 2009. URL: http://www.navy.mil/search/display.asp?story_id=49242

72. U.S. House Committee on Energy and Commerce. *H.R. 2454: To create clean energy jobs, achieve energy independence, reduce global warming pollution and transition to a clean energy economy. (Also referred to as "the American Clean Energy and Security Act of 2009").* 111th Congress, 1st session. Washington, DC, May 21, 2009. URL: http://energycommerce.house.gov/Press_111/20090701/hr2454_house.pdf

73. U.S. House Committee on Ways and Means. *H.R. 1337: To amend the Internal Revenue Code of 1986 to reduce carbon dioxide emissions in the United States domestic energy supply. (Also referred to as "America's Energy Security Trust Fund Act of 2009").* 111th Congress, 1st session. Washington, DC, March 5, 2009. URL: http://frwebgate.access.gpo.gov/cgi-bin/getdoc.cgi?dbname=111_cong_bills&docid=f:h1337ih.txt.pdf

74. USTDA. "Clean Energy Development in China Offers New Export Opportunities for U.S. Technology Companies: USTDA Director Zak Encourages U.S.-China Energy Cooperation". United States Trade and Development Agency. Arlington, VA, May 21, 2010. URL: http://www.ustda.gov/news/pressreleases/2010/EastAsia/China/ChinaCleanEnergy_052110.pdf

ABOUT CITIZENS CLIMATE LOBBY

Citizens Climate Lobby is a national non-partisan, non-profit organization, working to organize citizen volunteers, by state, county or Congressional district, to lobby elected officials for a strong emissions reduction plan that will prevent catastrophic climate change and speed the transition to clean energy. The group aims to motivate political support, across the political spectrum, for a pragmatic approach to emissions reduction and to speeding the transition to clean energy.

The CCL strategy entails reaching out to all members of Congress, in both parties, regardless of their specific views or past staunch opposition to carbon-reduction legislation. The aim is to listen, to understand what specific elected officials and their constituencies most value and how they prioritize issues of energy and climate, and to work with them to help them achieve their goals in a way that is consistent with establishing a sustainable, responsible climate policy.

CCL also publishes position papers on issues relating to climate change mitigation, carbon pricing and strategies for reducing carbon-dioxide emissions.

For more information, visit: www.citizensclimatelobby.org

ABOUT THE AUTHOR

Joseph Robertson is a writer, editor, and educator, as well as founder and director of TheHotSpring.net, a social networking project that aims to bring people together from around the world and across disciplines, to achieve paradigm-shift innovations in policy and technology that can be used to help build a cleaner, more sustainable and more just future.

He has published three books of poetry in Spanish and is currently a Visiting Instructor of Spanish-language and Humanities at Villanova University, where he is assistant director of the online magazine *Naufragios*.

He is a volunteer for Citizens Climate Lobby, and for years contributed translations into Spanish for the Earth Policy Institute's eco-economy and *Plan B* updates online. He has written extensively on issues of ecological economics and is preparing a book examining questions of generative economic capacity, the degree to which economic activities are capable of expanding the resource base, instead of depleting it.

For more information, visit: www.thehotspring.net

CPSIA information can be obtained at www.ICGtesting.com
Printed in the USA
LVOW040752040512

280200LV00001B/3/P